1000 Ideas
for Colour Schemes

1000 Ideas for Colour Schemes

The ultimate guide to making colours work

Jennifer Ott

APPLE PRESS

A QUARTO BOOK

First published in the UK in 2016 by
Apple Press
74–77 White Lion Street
London N1 9PF

www.apple-press.com

Copyright © 2016 Quarto plc

ISBN: 978-1-84543-663-6

QUAR.CLRS

Conceived, designed and produced by
Quarto Publishing plc
The Old Brewery
6 Blundell Street
London N7 9BH

www.quartoknows.com

Senior Editor: Lily de Gatacre
Picture Researcher: Mahina Drew
Proofreader: Caroline West
Indexer: Helen Snaith
Art Director: Caroline Guest

Creative Director: Moira Clinch
Publisher: Paul Carslake

Colour separation in Hong Kong by Bright Arts Ltd
Printed in China by C & C Offset Printing Co Ltd

9 8 7 6 5 4 3 2 1

Contents

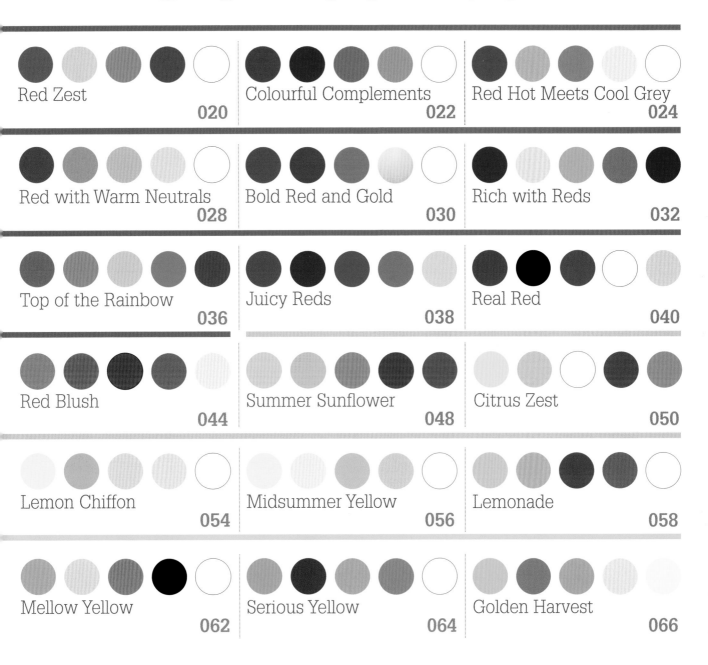

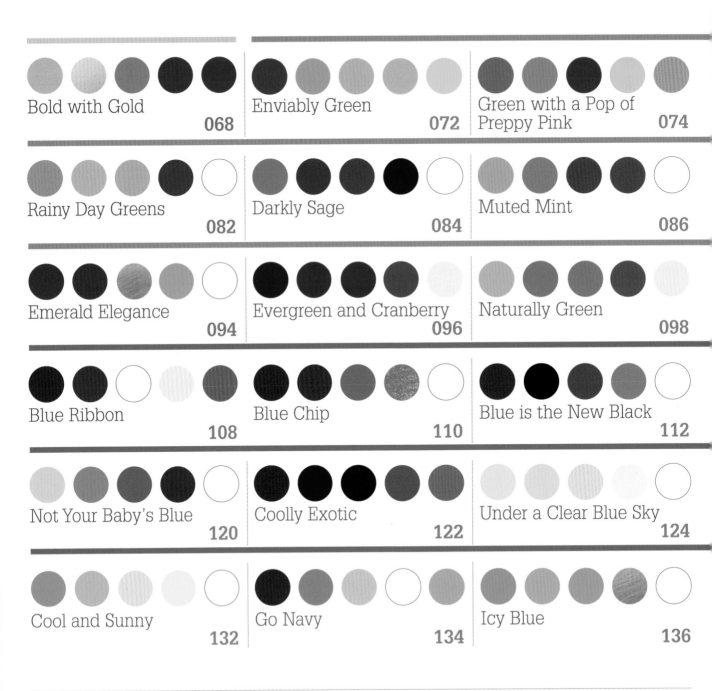

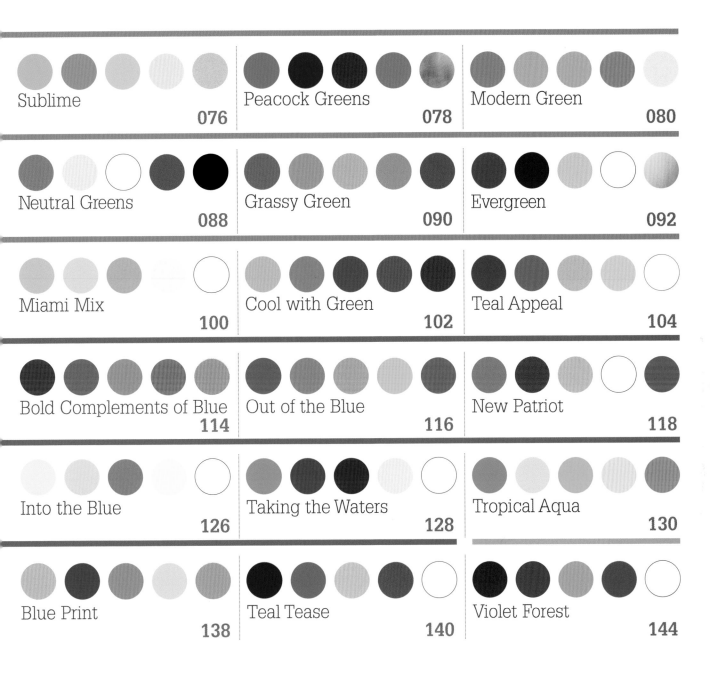

Sublime
076

Peacock Greens
078

Modern Green
080

Neutral Greens
088

Grassy Green
090

Evergreen
092

Miami Mix
100

Cool with Green
102

Teal Appeal
104

Bold Complements of Blue
114

Out of the Blue
116

New Patriot
118

Into the Blue
126

Taking the Waters
128

Tropical Aqua
130

Blue Print
138

Teal Tease
140

Violet Forest
144

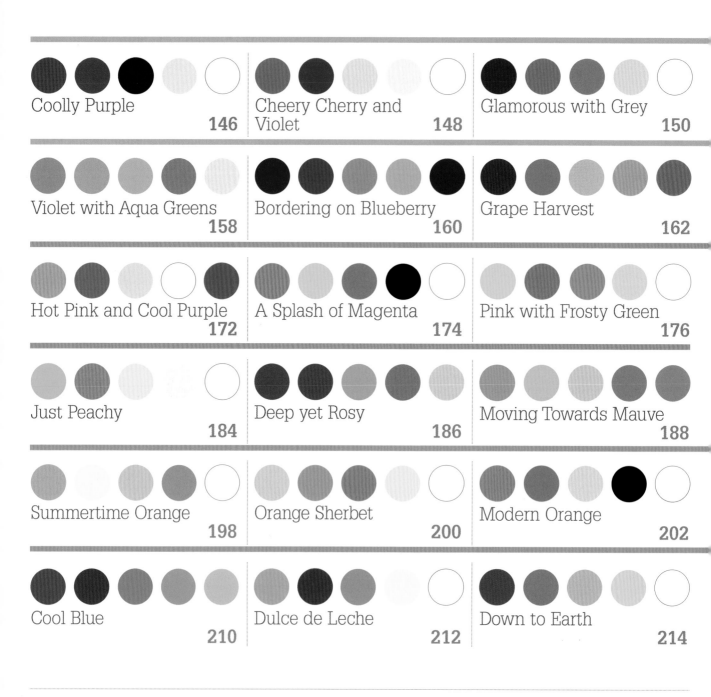

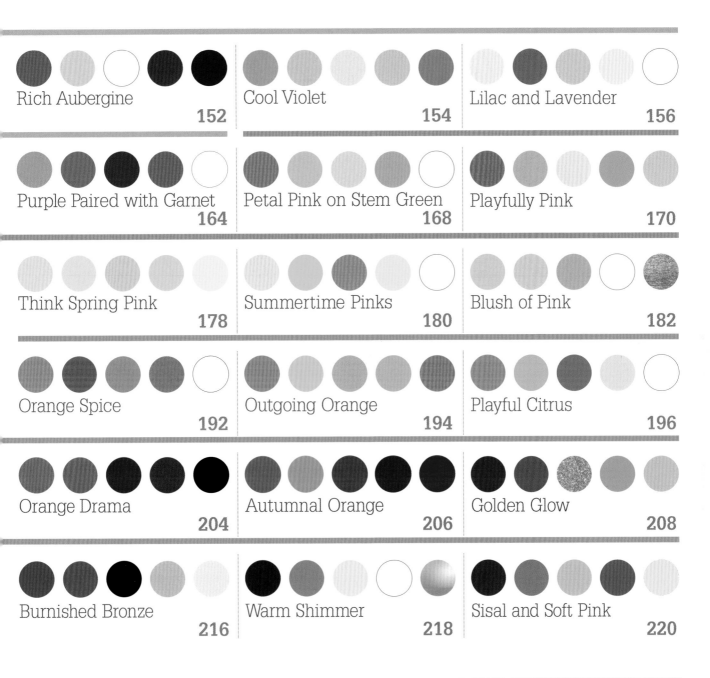

Rich Aubergine
152

Cool Violet
154

Lilac and Lavender
156

Purple Paired with Garnet
164

Petal Pink on Stem Green
168

Playfully Pink
170

Think Spring Pink
178

Summertime Pinks
180

Blush of Pink
182

Orange Spice
192

Outgoing Orange
194

Playful Citrus
196

Orange Drama
204

Autumnal Orange
206

Golden Glow
208

Burnished Bronze
216

Warm Shimmer
218

Sisal and Soft Pink
220

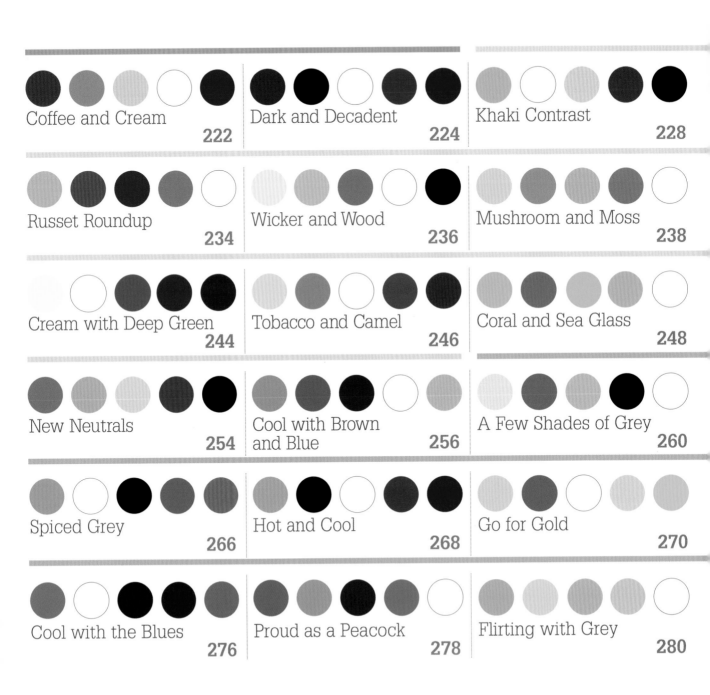

"Listen to the colour of your dreams."

The Beatles

Our lives today are saturated with colours.

Printed, dyed, painted, tinted, stained, digital, synthetic or natural – we are continuously bombarded with colour in everything we do. So, when it comes to choosing colours, the options on offer can be rather overwhelming. From paint charts in DIY stores to online colour cards and fabric charts, we are completely spoilt for choice.

I have worked in the field of colour and design for more than twenty years. I work closely with clothing designers, homeware manufacturers, hoteliers and creative people who are developing new products. Even colour and design experts find it hard to choose colours!

Part of the problem is the sheer amount of colour inspiration that exists in our world today. It is endless. Part of what I do is to 'decipher the rainbow' – to work through all of the inspiration on offer and choose the right colours for the right products, materials and surfaces. My job is to create beautiful books and colour combinations that help brands, retailers and designers to make the right colour choices. I am passionate about getting designers to think creatively. In our modern world we are truly overloaded with visual inspiration and new ideas or colour trends so my advice to everyone – whether the CEO of a large clothing retailer or a friend picking paint colours for her bathroom – is listen to your heart and choose colours that you instinctively love.

We all have a favourite colour or group of colours that we are drawn back to again and again. Whether you're getting dressed in the morning or decorating a table, colour plays a huge role in many choices we make every day of our lives. Every single person views colour in an individual way – we just know which colours we like or dislike. Believing in your own colour choices is the first step to creating your own personal sense of style!

It is books like this that help us to transform our favourite colours into our dream colour schemes. It is not an easy thing to create great colour combinations or choose the perfect accent shades to complement a colour scheme; the wrong tones of colour can clash or 'jar' against one another. But finding the perfect shades that suit and accentuate one another can turn a simple room into a space of beauty.

This book is stacked full of clever colour palettes and tons of beautiful, inspiring images, which will turn your colour decision-making process into a dream, rather than a nightmare!

Anna Starmer

Using this Book

This book is for anyone who loves colour and is looking for creative palettes they can incorporate into their surroundings, whether for home décor and apparel, or special events, parties and weddings.

Colour Selection Tip:

Most paint retailers can create a custom colour blend for you, so if you see a colour in this book that you would like translated into paint, simply take this book in to have the swatch colour-matched. Before committing to any paint colour it's always a good idea to paint up a test swatch to evaluate the hue in your own space, during different times of the day.

Sometimes you have an idea for a colour combination and just need to see a real-life example of the palette in action to make sure it works. Or perhaps you love a specific hue but are unsure of how to pair it with other colours to make it sing. Use this book to inspire you to think beyond the typical colour combinations. Whether or not you've got a specific colour in mind, use the visual contents on pages 4–11 to find a palette that jumps out at you and then locate it in the book. The ideas are grouped into nine colour families to give you some guidance, but the classifications are very fluid. When choosing a scheme, you don't have to include all of the colours that are shown in the palette. You might find a scheme that you love exactly as it is, which is great, but there's nothing wrong with tweaking and editing the colour palettes, using them as inspiration or focusing on just two or three of the colours to create something wonderful.

Alongside this book, get colour inspiration by collecting and organising examples of the colourful things you love. Whether it's swatches of paint or fabrics, or images culled from magazines or online sources, just clip and save what you're drawn to. You'll probably find a theme running through these assembled items, whether it's a specific colour or group of colours, a pattern or a material. Use these as the springboard from which you can further develop the colour scheme or design.

The Colour Wheel

This book requires no knowledge of colour theory, but a few basics about the colour wheel will help. For the purposes of this book we are referring to colour as it relates to paints, inks and dyes, rather than colour as a projection of light – such as how you see it on your computer monitor or television. When referring to pigments, then, there are three **primary colours:** red, yellow and blue. From these three primaries we can mix the **secondary colours** of orange, green and violet. Additionally, there are **tertiary colours** mixed from the primaries and secondaries: red-orange, yellow-orange, yellow-green, blue-green, blue-violet and red-violet. These twelve colours form the basic colour wheel.

Complementary colours are colours that are opposite one another on the colour wheel, the main combinations being blue and orange; red and

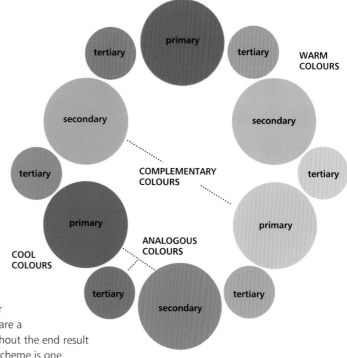

green; and yellow and violet. They offer the maximum amount of contrast to one another, and each makes the other appear more vibrant. This tension creates an energetic, dynamic colour combination. **Analogous colours** are hues that sit next to one another on the colour wheel. They tend to offer a pleasing, harmonious vibe and are a great way to employ an assortment of different colours without the end result appearing too garish. An example of an analogous colour scheme is one inspired by the sea, featuring various shades of blue, blue-green and green.

A couple of other characteristics of colour to consider are value and chroma. **Value** refers to the relative lightness or darkness of a colour. When white is added to a hue it is said to be a high-value colour, and is referred to as a **tint**. Add black to a hue to create a **shade**, a low-value colour. When grey is added to a hue it creates a mid-value colour, and is referred to as a **tone**. **Chroma**, also known as intensity or saturation, has to do with the purity of colour. A blue with a good amount of grey in it is going to appear much less saturated than pure primary blue. You can also desaturate a colour by mixing in a small bit of its complement colour. Low-saturation colours tend to have a more natural and subdued quality to them.

Finally, you'll often see colours in this book referred to as either 'warm' or 'cool'. The **cool colours** on the colour wheel run from yellow-green to violet. These hues have a calming, relaxing vibe. They also tend to visually recede, so when used in the home they can make a room feel larger and more expansive. The **warm colours** run from red-violet to yellow. These are happy, high-energy colours. In a home's interior they visually advance and can make a space feel more cosy and intimate.

'Use this book to inspire you to think beyond the typical colour combinations.'

red

Black, White, and Red All Over

Give a classic black and white scheme a boost through the addition of lush reds. Keep things light and bright by using white or light grey as the main colour. If you prefer a bold, graphic look, up the red or black elements.

RED

YELLOW

GREEN

BLUE

VIOLET

PINK

ORANGE
& BROWN

NEUTRAL

GREY

Red Zest

Spicy, citrusy hues are a natural fit with red. These colours are all adjacent to one another on the warmer side of the colour wheel, so although they are wildly colourful, they also have a harmonious flavour when used together.

RED

YELLOW

GREEN

BLUE

VIOLET

PINK

ORANGE
& BROWN

NEUTRAL

GREY

Colourful Complements

This festive palette features complementary colours red and green. When working with complementary hues, it's best to use one of the colours in small doses, or pick a muted version of it, so that the hues don't fight with one another.

RED

YELLOW

GREEN

BLUE

VIOLET

PINK

ORANGE
& BROWN

NEUTRAL

GREY

Red Hot Meets Cool Grey

Chill out with red by giving it a grey counterpoint. This mix of hot and cool feels balanced, ultra-modern and very sophisticated. Select sparkling pewter or silver elements for an especially elegant touch.

RED
YELLOW
GREEN
BLUE
VIOLET
PINK
ORANGE & BROWN
NEUTRAL
GREY

Opposites Attract

Red-orange and blue-green are complementary colours, opposites on the colour wheel, so they amp up each other's vibrancy. Pairing these contrasting hues with black and white produces a youthful, high-octane, attention-grabbing palette.

RED

YELLOW

GREEN

BLUE

VIOLET

PINK

ORANGE
& BROWN

NEUTRAL

GREY

Red with Warm Neutrals

True red is truly bold, but if you pair it with fellow warm hues, especially those of the soft, neutral variety, you can tone down the impact of the revved-up red. A touch of soft grey gives the palette a modern edge.

Bold Red and Gold

Red represents strength, vigour and passion, whereas gold conveys optimism, success and extravagance. When used in concert, the two make a powerful statement. Both are strong hues, so use one more sparingly than the other.

RED

YELLOW

GREEN

BLUE

VIOLET

PINK

ORANGE
& BROWN

NEUTRAL

GREY

Rich with Reds

Red-wine hues get an indulgent kiss of caramel in this handsome colour scheme.
It's the perfect palette for a bedroom or dining room – where a cosy and intimate
ambience is desired. In fashion, the hues convey a sophisticated and confident vibe.

RED

YELLOW

GREEN

BLUE

VIOLET

PINK

ORANGE & BROWN

NEUTRAL

GREY

Tawny Tones

These handsome, toned-down reds have strong brown and orange undertones, which give them a neutral quality. A rich and spicy palette like this works well for autumn occasions, or for décor in homes located in cold climates.

RED

YELLOW

GREEN

BLUE

VIOLET

PINK

ORANGE
& BROWN

NEUTRAL

GREY

Top of the Rainbow

This colourful palette shouts with glee and calls for a party. Use it when a fun and lighthearted look is in order. It's a delightful scheme for a child's recreational space, or send it outside to play in the sunshine, which helps moderate the vividness.

RED

YELLOW

GREEN

BLUE

VIOLET

PINK

ORANGE & BROWN

NEUTRAL

GREY

Juicy Reds

Succulent strawberry, cherry and raspberry reds form a deliciously decadent palette. Such luscious colours pair well with a darker, punctuating hue such as crisp blue-grey. A dash of spring green lends a fresh element.

Real Red

A high-saturation red hue is sexy, exciting and always eye-catching. Allow it to take centre stage by pairing it with solid, supporting neutrals. Black, dark grey, warm white and pure white hues form a solid foundation from which red can really sizzle.

RED
YELLOW
GREEN
BLUE
VIOLET
PINK
ORANGE & BROWN
NEUTRAL
GREY

Hint of Red

Tame an aggressive hue such as red either by using it in small amounts or by selecting a less-saturated version of it. Red tints (red with white added), tones (red with grey added) and shades (red with black added) have a softer quality than true red.

RED

YELLOW

GREEN

BLUE

VIOLET

PINK

ORANGE
& BROWN

NEUTRAL

GREY

Red Blush

Soft and slightly faded red-orange colours have a timeless elegance. These subdued copper and terracotta hues flatter a variety of skin tones, so they form a pleasing colour scheme to surround oneself with, whether through fashion or décor.

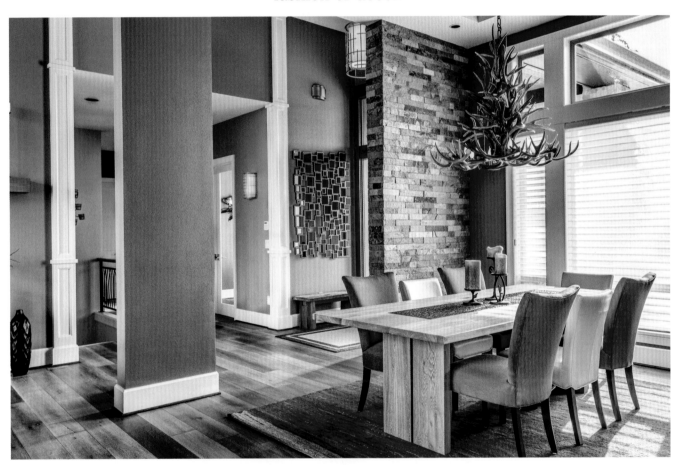

RED

YELLOW

GREEN

BLUE

VIOLET

PINK

ORANGE
& BROWN

NEUTRAL

GREY

yellow

Summer Sunflower

Vivid yellows and oranges join forces with a deep maroon and leafy green for a colour scheme inspired by late-summer flowers. This is a lively palette that conjures up happy, joyful times.

RED

YELLOW

GREEN

BLUE

VIOLET

PINK

ORANGE
& BROWN

NEUTRAL

GREY

Citrus Zest

Turn to nature for a pleasing
and stress-easing colour palette.
Whether inspired by the flowers in
bloom or a display of fresh produce
at the market, these big juicy
colours delight the senses.

RED

YELLOW

GREEN

BLUE

VIOLET

PINK

ORANGE
& BROWN

NEUTRAL

GREY

The Sun in the Sky

Yellow suggests warm sunshine and these deep blue hues evoke the sea and the sky. When used together, these near-complementary colours pulled from the great outdoors form a fun and dynamic palette.

RED

YELLOW

GREEN

BLUE

VIOLET

PINK

ORANGE
& BROWN

NEUTRAL

GREY

Lemon Chiffon

Yellow can be tough to work with because it often comes on a bit too strong. Soften the impact by going with a tint – a yellow with white added. Muted yellow tints often work as neutrals in a colour palette.

RED

YELLOW

GREEN

BLUE

VIOLET

PINK

ORANGE
& BROWN

NEUTRAL

GREY

Midsummer Yellow

Transport yourself to the beach or poolside with a relaxed, sun-faded colour scheme. Yellow should be the cornerstone of any summer-themed palette. A soft sorbet yellow paired with mint and a touch of cooling blue is sublime.

Lemonade

Take a refreshing sip of this sweet and tart scheme. Yellows with green undertones bring a fresh and crisp vibe. They balance out heavier, murkier colours such as rum-raisin reds and deep emerald greens.

RED

YELLOW

GREEN

BLUE

VIOLET

PINK

ORANGE
& BROWN

NEUTRAL

GREY

Cool with Yellow

A simple, cool and elegant palette starts with a base layer of grey and black. From here you can jazz it up with a splash of electric yellow. Such dazzling yellows are best in small doses and partnered with neutrals.

RED

YELLOW

GREEN

BLUE

VIOLET

PINK

ORANGE
& BROWN

NEUTRAL

GREY

Mellow Yellow

Bring the vibrancy level down by selecting yellows that have a bit of grey or brown in them, which keeps them from appearing fluorescent. Adding red, white and black to the palette gives it a punchy, graphic vibe.

RED

YELLOW

GREEN

BLUE

VIOLET

PINK

ORANGE
& BROWN

NEUTRAL

GREY

Serious Yellow

Mustard yellow can be tricky to pull off due to its heavy brown undertones. Give it a fresh and modern boost by pairing it with steely blue-greys, as well as a healthy smattering of white.

RED

YELLOW

GREEN

BLUE

VIOLET

PINK

ORANGE
& BROWN

NEUTRAL

GREY

Golden Harvest

As yellow shifts to orange it takes on a soft glow reminiscent of the setting sun or ready-to-harvest wheat fields. Warm browns, tans and creams serve as supporting neutrals in this luminous colour scheme.

RED

YELLOW

GREEN

BLUE

VIOLET

PINK

ORANGE
& BROWN

NEUTRAL

GREY

Bold with Gold

This warm, rich palette features autumn's best hues. It's an ideal colour scheme for places and spaces in which a cosy, welcoming vibe is desired. Counteract the heaviness of the dark brown by including sparkling gold elements.

RED

YELLOW

GREEN

BLUE

VIOLET

PINK

ORANGE
& BROWN

NEUTRAL

GREY

green

Enviably Green

This fun, bold palette has an exotic vibe that is sure to spark a party atmosphere. Whether you are looking to stimulate appetites, conversations or good times, this tropically inspired scheme will keep the mood festive.

RED
YELLOW
GREEN
BLUE
VIOLET
PINK
ORANGE & BROWN
NEUTRAL
GREY

Green with a Pop of Preppy Pink

Pink and leafy green are complementary colours – opposite each other on the colour wheel. This means they offer the most contrast to one another. The best way to punch up a yellow-green scheme is with a little pop of pink.

RED

YELLOW

GREEN

BLUE

VIOLET

PINK

ORANGE
& BROWN

NEUTRAL

GREY

Sublime

Lime is a vibrant yellow-green that can stand all on its own or have its impact softened by a pairing with other more herbaceous greens, as well as a generous dose of soft blue-greys.

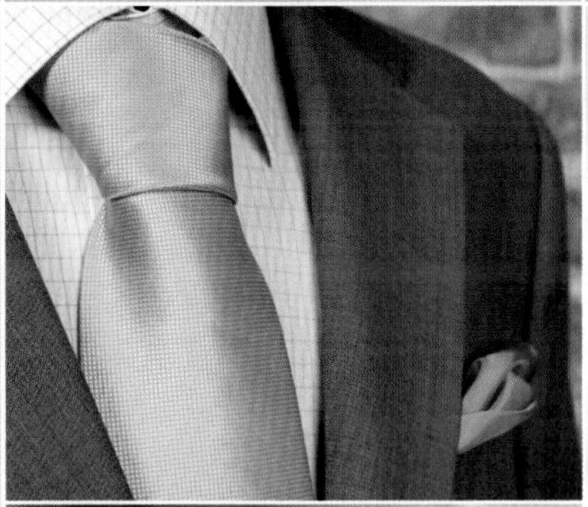

RED

YELLOW

GREEN

BLUE

VIOLET

PINK

ORANGE
& BROWN

NEUTRAL

GREY

Peacock Greens

Rich, peacock-inspired greens and blues form a bold, fashionable colour palette.
There's nothing soft or neutral about this scheme, so use it to call attention to
items that are worth putting in the limelight.

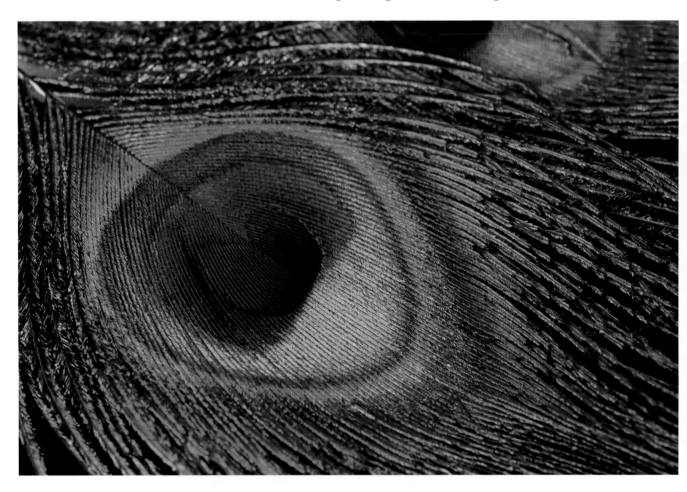

RED

YELLOW

GREEN

BLUE

VIOLET

PINK

ORANGE
& BROWN

NEUTRAL

GREY

Modern Green

Saturated greens play well with punchy citrus hues. It's a popular midcentury modern palette that continuously cycles back into vogue. These vibrant hues work best when one or two colours dominate, with the rest used as smaller accents.

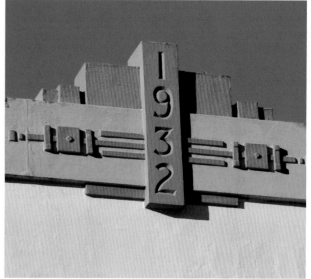

RED

YELLOW

GREEN

BLUE

VIOLET

PINK

ORANGE
& BROWN

NEUTRAL

GREY

Rainy Day Greens

Blue-green hues call to mind water, and when they have a touch of grey in them they acquire a restful and almost moody quality. Sharpen them up with accents of darker blue and pure white.

RED
YELLOW
GREEN
BLUE
VIOLET
PINK
ORANGE & BROWN
NEUTRAL
GREY

Darkly Sage

A cool green with a heavy grey undertone can be used as an alternative to the cast of usual neutrals – white, grey and beige. You can pair pretty much any colour you want with these dialed-down greens, making them super versatile.

RED

YELLOW

GREEN

BLUE

VIOLET

PINK

ORANGE
& BROWN

NEUTRAL

GREY

Muted Mint

This featured green has a good amount of grey in it, which softens and neutralises it. When partnered with a rich mahogany and a dark carbon grey, it forms a palette that is down-to-earth yet super elegant.

RED

YELLOW

GREEN

BLUE

VIOLET

PINK

ORANGE
& BROWN

NEUTRAL

GREY

Neutral Greens

Soft greens with a generous dose of either grey or brown can stand on their own as a neutral hue, or you can pair them with other neutrals for a palette that is toned down yet layered and interesting.

RED

YELLOW

GREEN

BLUE

VIOLET

PINK

ORANGE
& BROWN

NEUTRAL

GREY

Grassy Green

Fresh greens taken from nature have a youthful vibrancy. We associate them with hope, rebirth and renewal, so we tend to be drawn to them during times of crisis or uncertainty in the world.

RED

YELLOW

GREEN

BLUE

VIOLET

PINK

ORANGE
& BROWN

NEUTRAL

GREY

Evergreen

These deep, dark, saturated greens need to be partnered with plenty of white or other light neutrals to keep the palette from becoming too sombre or heavy. But in small quantities, they look absolutely dashing.

Emerald Elegance

Dark and subdued, but in no way sombre, this deep, dark green makes a nice alternative to basic black or navy as the anchoring hue in a palette. Pair it with a rich red wine or camel hue to give the scheme a warm boost.

RED

YELLOW

GREEN

BLUE

VIOLET

PINK

ORANGE
& BROWN

NEUTRAL

GREY

Evergreen and Cranberry

True green and deep red are opposite one another on the colour wheel and therefore each magnifies the intensity of the other. This palette is a bit of an attention-grabber, but the deep and saturated quality of the hues offers a comforting vibe.

RED

YELLOW

GREEN

BLUE

VIOLET

PINK

ORANGE
& BROWN

NEUTRAL

GREY

Naturally Green

Greens with strong yellow and brown undertones feel very earthy and grounded. Layer them with other colours pulled from nature for a colourful yet soothing look, or jazz them up with splashes of more vibrant hues.

RED

YELLOW

GREEN

BLUE

VIOLET

PINK

ORANGE
& BROWN

NEUTRAL

GREY

Miami Mix

Not quite pastels, but also not fully saturated brights, these are colours that have been softened by exposure to the sun and salt air. This fun palette evokes warm sunny days near the beach and hot nights on the town.

RED

YELLOW

GREEN

BLUE

VIOLET

PINK

ORANGE
& BROWN

NEUTRAL

GREY

Cool with Green

For a colourful palette that retains a harmonious vibe, gather an assortment of colours from one end of the colour spectrum. Here we have a range of cool colours from blue-green to violet-red that flow smoothly into one another.

RED

YELLOW

GREEN

BLUE

VIOLET

PINK

ORANGE
& BROWN

NEUTRAL

GREY

Teal Appeal

Teal and golden yellow aren't quite complementary colours, but they do contrast with one another so that they coalesce into an energetic, lively palette. Use one as a background to the other to set each element apart.

RED

YELLOW

GREEN

BLUE

VIOLET

PINK

ORANGE
& BROWN

NEUTRAL

GREY

blue

Blue Ribbon

True blue colours tend to recede visually, so they make a great background hue that allows other warmer colours to advance. When used inside a home they can help make a space feel more spacious and open.

RED

YELLOW

GREEN

BLUE

VIOLET

PINK

ORANGE
& BROWN

NEUTRAL

GREY

Blue Chip

Blue is associated with loyalty, trust and commitment. Gold elements call to mind wealth, opulence and decadence. This interesting combination of colours and meanings has an upscale, formal quality that evokes momentous occasions.

RED

YELLOW

GREEN

BLUE

VIOLET

PINK

ORANGE
& BROWN

NEUTRAL

GREY

Blue is the New Black

Enhance the classic elegance of black and charcoal grey with the addition of inky indigo hues. Keep the scheme airy and light through the use of plenty of white and soft grey. For more drama, up the amount of deep, dark hues.

RED

YELLOW

GREEN

BLUE

VIOLET

PINK

ORANGE
& BROWN

NEUTRAL

GREY

Bold Complements of Blue

Blue and orange are complementary colours, or colour wheel contrasts. They are best used when an exciting, high-energy look is desired. One way to make it more mellow is to use one or both of the hues in small amounts only.

RED

YELLOW

GREEN

BLUE

VIOLET

PINK

ORANGE
& BROWN

NEUTRAL

GREY

Out of the Blue

This palette is for enthusiastic lovers of colour. A sampling of more than half of the colour wheel (from orange to yellow to green to blue), it's a vivid scheme that should be reserved for occasions or items worthy of one's individual attention.

RED

YELLOW

GREEN

BLUE

VIOLET

PINK

ORANGE
& BROWN

NEUTRAL

GREY

New Patriot

Red, white and blue comprise the colours of the flag of many countries. Replace the royal or navy blue with toned-down shades of grey-blue for a fresh take on the palette. It's an unexpected scheme that has an understated appeal.

RED

YELLOW

GREEN

BLUE

VIOLET

PINK

ORANGE
& BROWN

NEUTRAL

GREY

Not Your Baby's Blue

If you prefer muted blues but don't want a palette of pastels, select blue tones (blue mixed with grey) or shades (blue mixed with black). The touch of grey or black softens the chroma, or purity, of the colour, giving the colours more of a neutral quality.

RED

YELLOW

GREEN

BLUE

VIOLET

PINK

ORANGE
& BROWN

NEUTRAL

GREY

Coolly Exotic

Hot pinks and cool blue-violets merge to form a hip, bohemian palette. This gorgeous scheme makes a striking statement. Use the bolder hues and the contrast between the colours to set off items worthy of being in the limelight.

RED

YELLOW

GREEN

BLUE

VIOLET

PINK

ORANGE
& BROWN

NEUTRAL

GREY

Under a Clear Blue Sky

Light sky blues offer the gentlest wisp of colour. To maintain a delicate touch, combine them with soft pastels such as pink and plenty of white. It's a sweet and innocent palette that's perfect for children's spaces and springtime celebrations.

RED

YELLOW

GREEN

BLUE

VIOLET

PINK

ORANGE
& BROWN

NEUTRAL

GREY

Into the Blue

A generous helping of pretty, soft blues has an airy and ethereal quality. When used in architectural applications, it exudes a cheerful sea- and sky-kissed vibe. In fashion and décor, it's fun and lighthearted, never to be taken too seriously.

RED
YELLOW
GREEN
BLUE
VIOLET
PINK
ORANGE
& BROWN
NEUTRAL
GREY

Taking the Waters

Watery blue colours can help us feel calm, soothed and relaxed. Up the energy level by increasing the vibrancy of one or more of the blue hues. It will still have a replenishing vibe, just with a bit more pep.

RED

YELLOW

GREEN

BLUE

VIOLET

PINK

ORANGE
& BROWN

NEUTRAL

GREY

Tropical Aqua

Bold blues with green undertones take us to warm and exotic places, especially when partnered with cheerful corals and pinks. This fun and vivacious colour scheme is ready for a party.

RED

YELLOW

GREEN

BLUE

VIOLET

PINK

ORANGE & BROWN

NEUTRAL

GREY

Cool and Sunny

Pool-blue hues mixed with golden sunshine yellows take us outdoors for some summertime fun. This can be a rather bold palette when used inside the home. You can rein it in by using one of the vibrant colours as a small accent only.

RED
YELLOW
GREEN
BLUE
VIOLET
PINK
ORANGE & BROWN
NEUTRAL
GREY

Go Navy

The darkest hues of blue have a handsome quality, but they can also feel a bit serious. Lighten them up with softer blue-greys and white. The addition of soft caramel or warm wood tones helps take the chill off.

RED
YELLOW
GREEN
BLUE
VIOLET
PINK
ORANGE & BROWN
NEUTRAL
GREY

Icy Blue

Blue is a natural fit with cool grey hues and metallic silver elements. This palette can feel a bit cold, so it's the perfect choice for homes in hot climates. In fashion it has a luxurious and elegant air without veering towards heavy or severe.

RED

YELLOW

GREEN

BLUE

VIOLET

PINK

ORANGE
& BROWN

NEUTRAL

GREY

Blue Print

Blue and green are side-by-side on the colour wheel, so they play together
nicely due to their similarity. Mix up a batch of beautiful true blue and
green-blue colours for a subtly colourful palette.

RED

YELLOW

GREEN

BLUE

VIOLET

PINK

ORANGE
& BROWN

NEUTRAL

GREY

Teal Tease

Deep blues with strong green undertones have an appealing, elegant air.
They're an excellent choice when a rich yet unconventional colour is desired.
When paired with cool, steely greys, they give a youthful, modern vibe.

RED

YELLOW

GREEN

BLUE

VIOLET

PINK

ORANGE
& BROWN

NEUTRAL

GREY

violet

Violet Forest

When working with bold, juicy purples, take inspiration from a bouquet of beautiful flowers and include plenty of leafy greens. These green hues bring a soothing organic vibe to the palette and help to ground the bright dashes of purple.

RED

YELLOW

GREEN

BLUE

VIOLET

PINK

ORANGE
& BROWN

NEUTRAL

GREY

Coolly Purple

A blue-tinged purple looks sharp when paired with classic navy. The colours are quite similar, so they flow into one another seamlessly. A splash of magenta adds warmth and vibrancy to the palette.

Cheery Cherry and Violet

This is a rich, vibrant colour palette, worthy of a special occasion. Balance out the bold purple and reds by adding a small dash of violet's complementary colour: yellow. Some white space also provides a visual breather.

RED

YELLOW

GREEN

BLUE

VIOLET

PINK

ORANGE
& BROWN

NEUTRAL

GREY

Glamorous with Grey

Flat grey hues tend to impart a modern, industrial vibe. Add a beguiling boost
of lilac to the colour scheme to soften it up and make it more special.
Enhancing with texture and sheen will also bring this palette to life.

RED

YELLOW

GREEN

BLUE

VIOLET

PINK

ORANGE
& BROWN

NEUTRAL

GREY

Rich Aubergine

Deep, dark and dashing, this hue is a warmer alternative to black or navy. A soft, silvery lilac adds a layer of lightness that keeps the palette from feeling too heavy or sombre.

RED

YELLOW

GREEN

BLUE

VIOLET

PINK

ORANGE
& BROWN

NEUTRAL

GREY

Cool Violet

Violet, blue and green are analogous colours, meaning they are next to one another on the colour wheel. Because of the similarity of hues, they feel harmonious when used together, despite the kaleidoscope of different colours.

RED

YELLOW

GREEN

BLUE

VIOLET

PINK

ORANGE
& BROWN

NEUTRAL

GREY

Lilac and Lavender

Soft, soothing light violet hues are thought to reduce feelings of stress and anxiety, so they are a terrific choice for home interiors. In fashion they have a cool, ethereal quality that can either be dressed up or down.

RED

YELLOW

GREEN

BLUE

VIOLET

PINK

ORANGE
& BROWN

NEUTRAL

GREY

Violet with Aqua Greens

Though not quite complementary colours, this collection of cool lilacs and violets with splashy aquas offers a vibrant palette option. This attention-getting scheme is best reserved for spaces, places and objects deserving of the spotlight.

RED

YELLOW

GREEN

BLUE

VIOLET

PINK

ORANGE
& BROWN

NEUTRAL

GREY

Bordering on Blueberry

Bold hues can sometimes fight with one another, but these purples and greens all have strong blue undertones, so when partnered with true blue, they feel harmonious and cohesive despite the use of highly saturated colours.

RED

YELLOW

GREEN

BLUE

VIOLET

PINK

ORANGE
& BROWN

NEUTRAL

GREY

Grape Harvest

Autumnal yellow-orange hues serve as a dramatic backdrop to deep grape colours. These nearly complementary hues sit in strong contrast to one another, forming a dynamic colour scheme. Ease the energy level by including some toned-down violets.

RED YELLOW GREEN BLUE VIOLET PINK ORANGE & BROWN NEUTRAL GREY

Purple Paired with Garnet

Gather up your favourite violet and red-violet hues for a beautiful, romantic colour scheme. The deeper plum colours really stand out against the softer, silvery lavender hues without looking too busy or severe.

RED

YELLOW

GREEN

BLUE

VIOLET

PINK

ORANGE
& BROWN

NEUTRAL

GREY

pink

Petal Pink on Stem Green

Look to nature for pink inspiration. Pretty petal pinks are right at home atop fresh, leafy greens. Pink and light green are complementary colours and, when used together, they pump up the vibrancy of one another.

RED

YELLOW

GREEN

BLUE

VIOLET

PINK

ORANGE
& BROWN

NEUTRAL

GREY

Playfully Pink

Red, blue and yellow are triadic colours – they are evenly spaced on the colour wheel. They form a high-contrast, high-energy colour palette. Using lighter shades of the hues will tone down the intensity of the palette while retaining the fun factor.

RED

YELLOW

GREEN

BLUE

VIOLET

PINK

ORANGE & BROWN

NEUTRAL

GREY

Hot Pink and Cool Purple

An assortment of pleasing pinks and purples unite for an enchanting colour scheme. The saturated pink hues give the palette a sophisticated vibe, whereas softer pinks veer it towards a more youthful look.

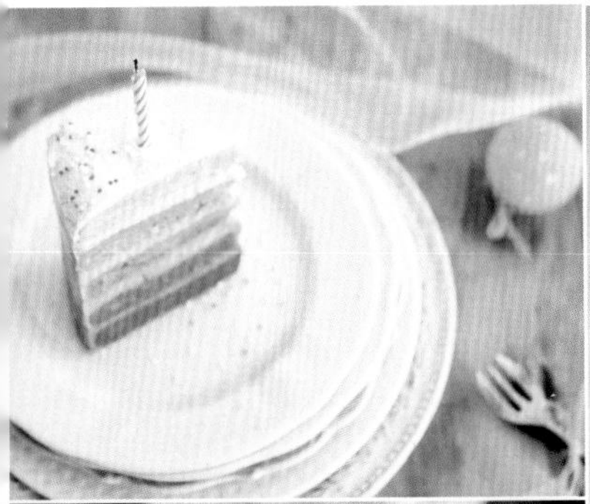
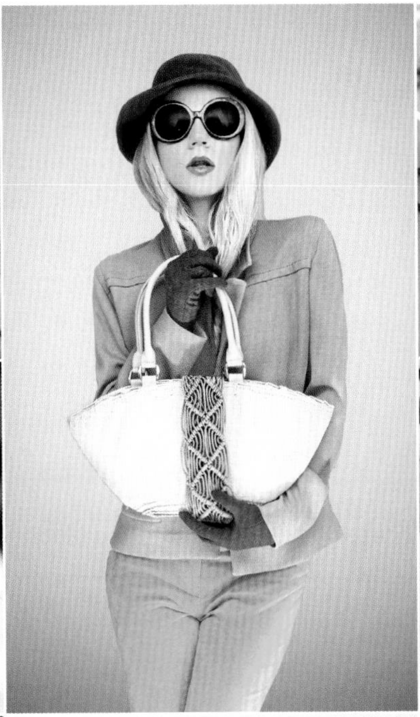
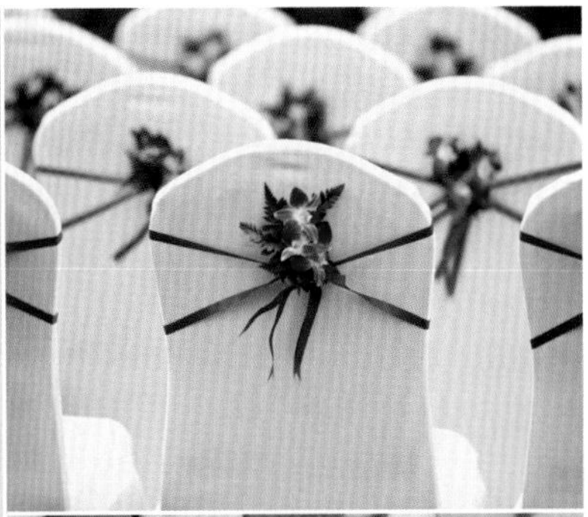
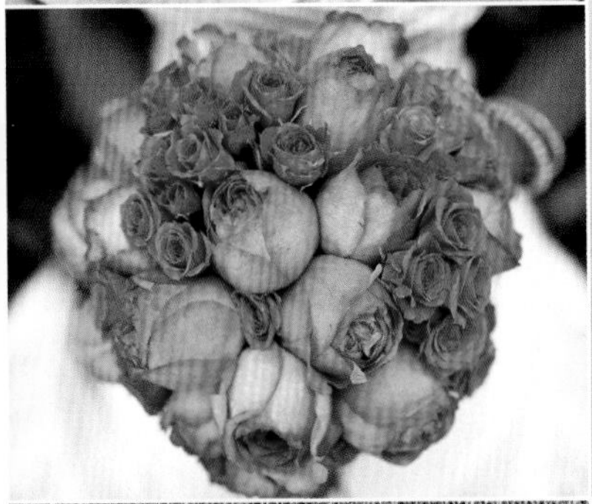
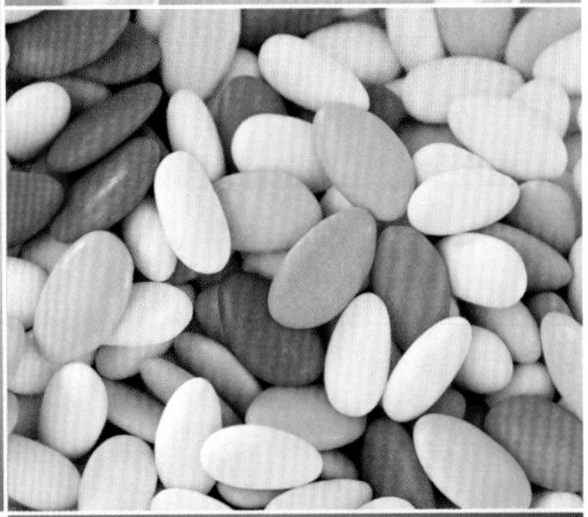
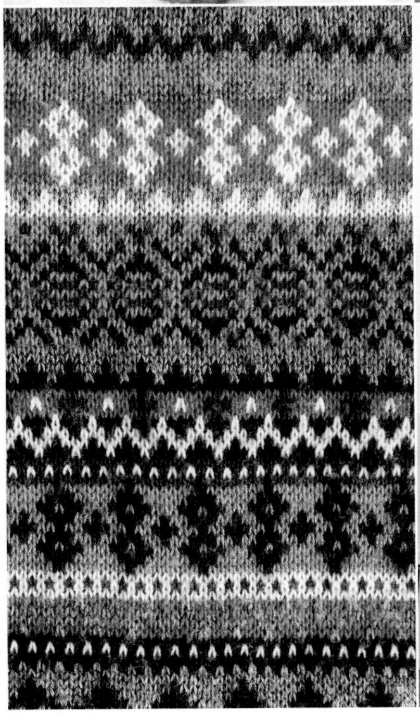
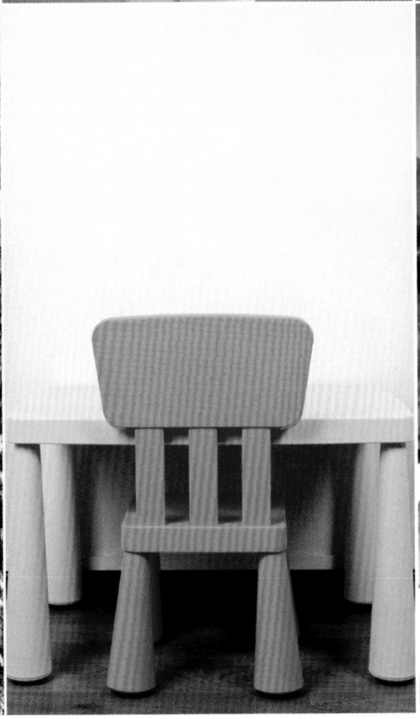
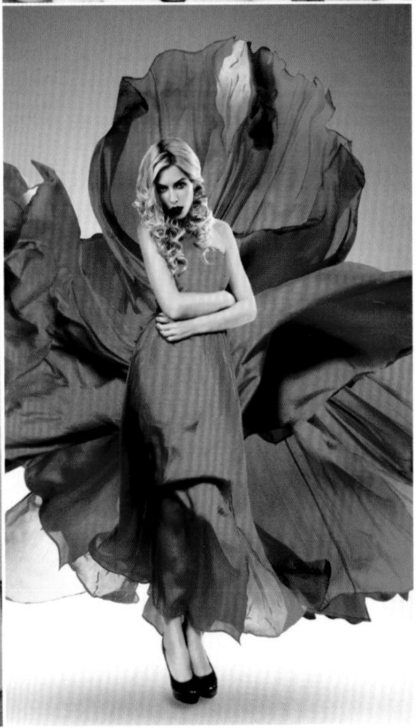

A Splash of Magenta

These pinks are not mere wallflower hues. So, although black and other dark neutrals can be used to form the basis of an elegant palette, a small injection of bold pink offers an unexpected boost of chic vivacity.

RED

YELLOW

GREEN

BLUE

VIOLET

PINK

ORANGE
& BROWN

NEUTRAL

GREY

Pink with Frosty Green

Layers of punchy pinks are always going to be the life of the party. Offer the eye a visual break by adding some contrasting silvery greens, then mix in plenty of white for a fetching palette that has a nice vintage feel.

RED

YELLOW

GREEN

BLUE

VIOLET

PINK

ORANGE
& BROWN

NEUTRAL

GREY

Think Spring Pink

A rainbow of pretty pastels heralds springtime and its hopeful sentiments of rebirth and renewal. The key to making this palette work is to look for colours that are of a similar value (lightness or darkness) and tint (amount of white added to the hue).

RED

YELLOW

GREEN

BLUE

VIOLET

PINK

ORANGE
& BROWN

NEUTRAL

GREY

Summertime Pinks

A batch of sweet pinks gets a warm boost from summer-sun yellow. This palette has a fun, youthful vibrancy. These are the happy hues of a season in full bloom and long days spent frolicking in the warm sunshine.

RED

YELLOW

GREEN

BLUE

VIOLET

PINK

ORANGE
& BROWN

NEUTRAL

GREY

Blush of Pink

A light seashell pink has a soft, breathy quality that you can make instantly elegant by pairing it with soft neutrals and metallic hues. A super-subtle palette such as this relies on interesting textiles to really make it sing.

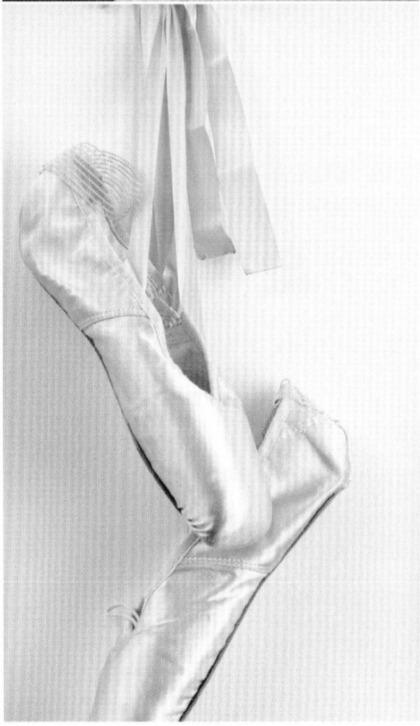

RED

YELLOW

GREEN

BLUE

VIOLET

PINK

ORANGE
& BROWN

NEUTRAL

GREY

Just Peachy

Fruit-inspired hues exude a sweet, comforting vibe. These pinks, peaches and soft yellows are analogous colours, so although they pack a punch, they do it in a harmonious way. Up the elegance factor by including sparkling silver or pearlescent elements.

RED

YELLOW

GREEN

BLUE

VIOLET

PINK

ORANGE & BROWN

NEUTRAL

GREY

Deep yet Rosy

Here's a pink-based colour scheme for anyone looking to ditch the pastels. A rich, dark rose hue can work as a neutral in a colourful palette, especially when partnered with fellow toned-down colours.

RED

YELLOW

GREEN

BLUE

VIOLET

PINK

ORANGE
& BROWN

NEUTRAL

GREY

Moving Towards Mauve

There's nothing babyish about this pink. A touch of grey knocks down the intensity, rendering it a little less sweet and innocent. This toned-down pink brings a welcome dash of warmth and spice to a palette full of similar moody, tonal hues.

RED

YELLOW

GREEN

BLUE

VIOLET

PINK

ORANGE
& BROWN

NEUTRAL

GREY

orange

& brown

Orange Spice

These brown-tinged oranges are spicy yet earthy. A foolproof way to pick a pleasingly colourful orange scheme is to select oranges that are of a similar value (lightness or darkness) and chroma (purity of colour).

RED

YELLOW

GREEN

BLUE

VIOLET

PINK

ORANGE
& BROWN

NEUTRAL

GREY

Outgoing Orange

Colours on the warm side of the colour wheel (reds, oranges and yellows) give off a friendly, vivacious vibe, especially the bolder versions. Warm colours are said to encourage conversation so they are perfect for dining rooms and party décor.

RED

YELLOW

GREEN

BLUE

VIOLET

PINK

ORANGE
& BROWN

NEUTRAL

GREY

Playful Citrus

Herbaceous green can serve as a neutral, so don't be afraid to add a little orange zest to the mix. There's no need to go eye-searingly bold here; using more toned-down greens will balance out a fiery orange.

RED

YELLOW

GREEN

BLUE

VIOLET

PINK

ORANGE
& BROWN

NEUTRAL

GREY

Summertime Orange

Sun-faded colours have a soft, dreamy and pleasing quality. These aren't quite pastel hues, but rather the toned-down versions of the vibrant fresh fruit and floral colours of spring.

RED

YELLOW

GREEN

BLUE

VIOLET

PINK

ORANGE
& BROWN

NEUTRAL

GREY

Orange Sherbet

A bold orange, although beautiful and eye-catching, can be a bit much when used in large doses. Try pairing it with light, creamy oranges, as well as a generous portion of white, to help balance out the brightness.

RED

YELLOW

GREEN

BLUE

VIOLET

PINK

ORANGE
& BROWN

NEUTRAL

GREY

Modern Orange

Orange hues are traditionally paired with warm neutrals such as tan, beige and cream. For a modern twist, try partnering orange with cooler neutrals such as taupe and grey, as well as cool whites and blacks.

RED
YELLOW
GREEN
BLUE
VIOLET
PINK
ORANGE
& BROWN
NEUTRAL
GREY

Orange Drama

Inky blue-grey and basic black are handsome base colours that get a lively lift
when combined with pumpkin orange. Tints and shades of red-violet soften
the contrast and add a whimsical element.

RED

YELLOW

GREEN

BLUE

VIOLET

PINK

ORANGE
& BROWN

NEUTRAL

GREY

Autumnal Orange

The warm, rich colours of the changing leaves herald the autumn and a period of transition ahead. Keep the palette from getting too spooky by bringing in plenty of lively orange and red-orange hues.

RED

YELLOW

GREEN

BLUE

VIOLET

PINK

ORANGE
& BROWN

NEUTRAL

GREY

Golden Glow

As orange veers towards brown it can start to turn a bit muddy. Perk it up with warm metallic accents such as copper, bronze and gold. These monochromatic colour schemes are perfect for playing around with texture, sheen and pattern.

RED

YELLOW

GREEN

BLUE

VIOLET

PINK

ORANGE
& BROWN

NEUTRAL

GREY

Cool Blue

Orange and blue are complementary colours, or opposite each other on the colour wheel. When using complementary colours, keep in mind that they each make the other appear more intense. Try keeping one of the hues more toned down, like this orange-brown, if the other is vibrant like these turquoise shades.

RED
YELLOW
GREEN
BLUE
VIOLET
PINK
ORANGE
& BROWN
NEUTRAL
GREY

Dulce de Leche

Sweet caramel and butterscotch hues provide a tasty alternative to basic brown or black. Mix and match tints (colour mixed with white), tones (colour mixed with grey) and shades (colour mixed with black) for a palette that's colourful but understated.

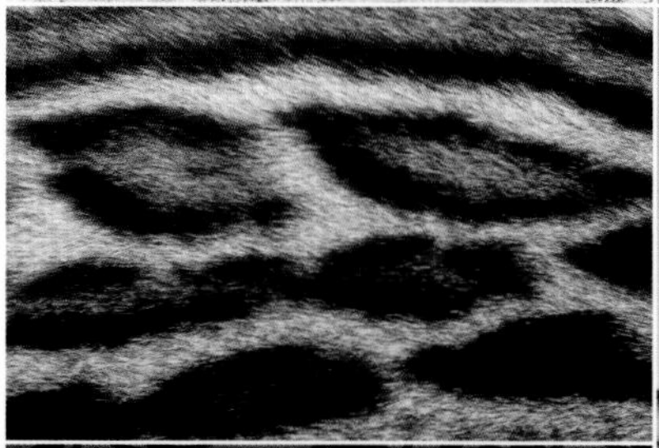

RED

YELLOW

GREEN

BLUE

VIOLET

PINK

ORANGE
& BROWN

NEUTRAL

GREY

Down to Earth

Rich brown hues inspired by nature have a pleasing, organic quality. From this earthy base, bring in a pretty accent such as a soft, blushing pink. This particular pink has orange undertones, which keep it from going too sugary sweet.

Burnished Bronze

Balance out cool, steely greys with warm, blackened bronze hues. Mixing warm tones with cool neutrals is a terrific way to bust out of an all-grey or all-beige rut. You can then add just about any fun accent colour that you like to this scheme.

RED
YELLOW
GREEN
BLUE
VIOLET
PINK
ORANGE & BROWN
NEUTRAL
GREY

Warm Shimmer

Typically, orange and brown hues are paired with warm metallic elements.
For a more modern approach, try partnering them with cool silver chromes
and steels. Polished metallic surfaces also amp up the elegance.

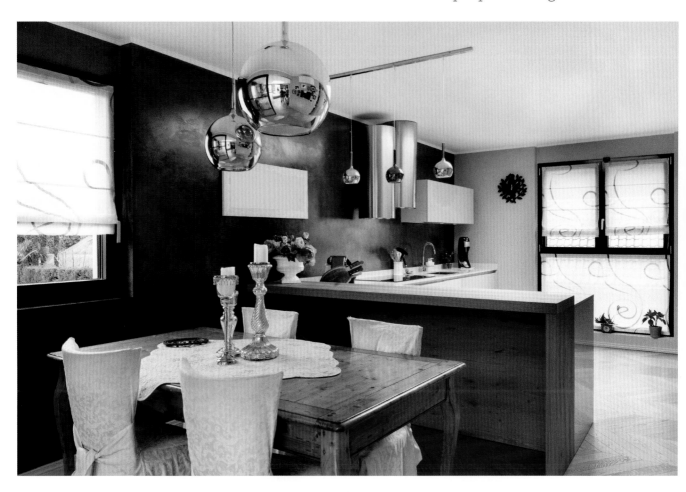

RED

YELLOW

GREEN

BLUE

VIOLET

PINK

ORANGE & BROWN

NEUTRAL

GREY

Sisal and Soft Pink

Colours pulled from natural fibres have a soft and casual quality, but with the added dash of shimmery pink, the palette takes on a dressier edge. It's an elegant palette that doesn't feel old or stuffy.

RED
YELLOW
GREEN
BLUE
VIOLET
PINK
ORANGE & BROWN
NEUTRAL
GREY

Coffee and Cream

This beautiful palette starts with a foundation of rich coffee hues – from a deep, dark espresso to a light café au lait – to which a generous dose of purple plum is introduced. The effect is glamorous without being too showy.

RED

YELLOW

GREEN

BLUE

VIOLET

PINK

ORANGE
& BROWN

NEUTRAL

GREY

Dark and Decadent

Delicious dark chocolate hues provide a rich base layer for a splash of deep cherry red. This sophisticated scheme is perfect for a dining room, library or master bedroom – spaces in which a cosy and intimate atmosphere is desired.

RED

YELLOW

GREEN

BLUE

VIOLET

PINK

ORANGE & BROWN

NEUTRAL

GREY

neutral

Khaki Contrast

Take khaki tan and pair it with contrasting light and dark hues for a neutral palette that has plenty of variety. The white keeps it light, and the dashes of dark brown and black add depth.

RED
YELLOW
GREEN
BLUE
VIOLET
PINK
ORANGE
& BROWN
NEUTRAL
GREY

Cinnamon Spice

Softly spicy hues impart a cosy and comforting ambience. A soft and harmonious palette such as this can handle shimmering elements, so consider amping up the glamour factor with the addition of warm metallic tones.

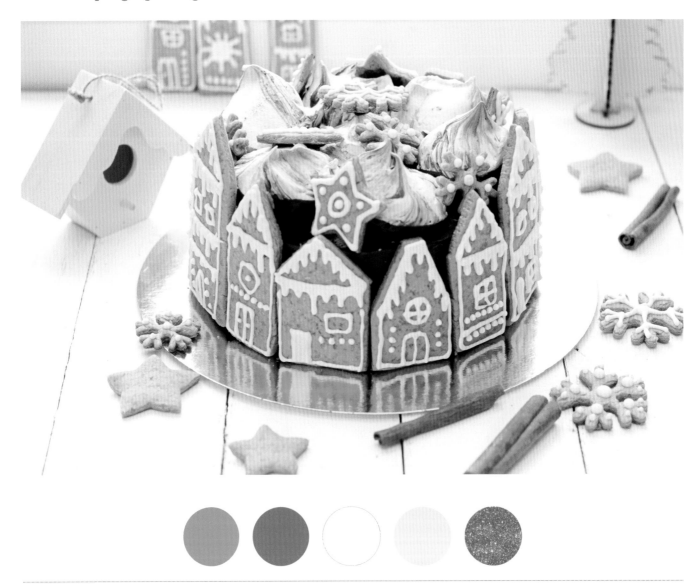

RED

YELLOW

GREEN

BLUE

VIOLET

PINK

ORANGE
& BROWN

NEUTRAL

GREY

A Better Beige

If you aren't a fan of ubiquitous beige and tan but haven't fully embraced grey either, give cooler shades of beige and tan a chance. These contain more grey than their warmer counterparts, giving them a fresh and modern air.

RED

YELLOW

GREEN

BLUE

VIOLET

PINK

ORANGE & BROWN

NEUTRAL

GREY

Russet Roundup

Highly saturated shades of warm hues such as red, orange and yellow can be visually noisy and overwhelming, especially when used in a home's interior. For a softer, more comforting vibe, go for toned-down versions of these hues.

RED

YELLOW

GREEN

BLUE

VIOLET

PINK

ORANGE
& BROWN

NEUTRAL

GREY

Wicker and Wood

A mix of browns – light and dark as well as warm and cool – unite for a rich, timeless palette. When working with a nearly monochromatic palette such as this, consider playing up texture, pattern and sheen.

RED

YELLOW

GREEN

BLUE

VIOLET

PINK

ORANGE
& BROWN

NEUTRAL

GREY

Mushroom and Moss

Nature arguably offers up some of the best colour palettes. Soft green and taupe hues abound in the natural world and so we tend to attach positive associations to them when we encounter them in other contexts.

RED
YELLOW
GREEN
BLUE
VIOLET
PINK
ORANGE & BROWN
NEUTRAL
GREY

Soft with Celery

Shake up a light and neutral palette with the addition of a crisp green hue. Greens with strong yellow undertones lend a fresh and cheery note. They're vibrant colours but also rather light in value, meaning they don't overwhelm.

RED

YELLOW

GREEN

BLUE

VIOLET

PINK

ORANGE
& BROWN

NEUTRAL

GREY

Brown Butterscotch

Predominantly white and off-white palettes have an airy and ethereal quality.
Ground the palette and add definition with the strategic inclusion of darker
hues, such as a rich brown or tonal orange.

RED

YELLOW

GREEN

BLUE

VIOLET

PINK

ORANGE & BROWN

NEUTRAL

GREY

Cream with Deep Green

Bring green out of the deep, dark forest and into a more formal and light-filled setting by partnering it with warm whites. These greens have slight blue undertones; the coolness they impart contrasts nicely with the soft warmth of the creams.

RED
YELLOW
GREEN
BLUE
VIOLET
PINK
ORANGE
& BROWN
NEUTRAL
GREY

Tobacco and Camel

These handsome, classic neutrals benefit from a nice wine pairing. The luscious burgundy helps to temper the slight muddiness of the main neutral colours. To retain its sense of specialness, use the burgundy as a small accent only.

RED

YELLOW

GREEN

BLUE

VIOLET

PINK

ORANGE
& BROWN

NEUTRAL

GREY

Coral and Sea Glass

Colourful palettes need not be overly bold and boisterous. Stick to a variety of soft, weathered hues for a neutral take on a colour-rich scheme. Dried-grass hues make a fantastic base for layers of soft coral and sea-glass green.

RED

YELLOW

GREEN

BLUE

VIOLET

PINK

ORANGE & BROWN

NEUTRAL

GREY

Berries and Chocolate

Surround yourself with the indulgent colours of your favourite comfort foods.
Vanilla, chocolate and berry-red hues rev up the appetite and invigorate the
senses, but they can also be used to add an air of contentment.

RED

YELLOW

GREEN

BLUE

VIOLET

PINK

ORANGE
& BROWN

NEUTRAL

GREY

Tonal Teal

Light and warm neutrals such as beige and tan tend to be popular go-to hues, especially in and on the home. Personalise the palette by including an accent of an unconventional colour, like a toned-down teal.

RED

YELLOW

GREEN

BLUE

VIOLET

PINK

ORANGE
& BROWN

NEUTRAL

GREY

New Neutrals

As beige and grey duke it out over the position of top neutral, consider other less common neutrals as alternatives. Shades of brown get a fresh twist with undertones of yellow and green. Navy blues can step up and fill in for black.

RED

YELLOW

GREEN

BLUE

VIOLET

PINK

ORANGE
& BROWN

NEUTRAL

GREY

Cool with Brown and Blue

Blue and orange are complementary colours, opposite each other on the colour wheel. When used together they form a lively, dynamic colour scheme. Tone down the energy level a notch by swapping orange for its more toned-down relation, brown.

RED

YELLOW

GREEN

BLUE

VIOLET

PINK

ORANGE
& BROWN

NEUTRAL

GREY

grey

A Few Shades of Grey

Monochromatic palettes have an air of quiet elegance, especially when the shades range from white to black. Play around with the grey a bit and use warm and cool shades together. This keeps the palette from feeling dreary or dull.

RED

YELLOW

GREEN

BLUE

VIOLET

PINK

ORANGE
& BROWN

NEUTRAL

GREY

Warmly Grey

Take the heavy edge off black and dark brown hues with a generous helping of a warm grey. This handsome scheme has a high-end vibe, especially with the addition of glimmering gold elements and details.

RED

YELLOW

GREEN

BLUE

VIOLET

PINK

ORANGE
& BROWN

NEUTRAL

GREY

Neutral Mix

Neither too hot nor too cold, this colour scheme gets it just right. Gather an assortment of warm and cool greys, and then add contrast with black and white. Tie it all together with a delectable dash of caramel.

RED

YELLOW

GREEN

BLUE

VIOLET

PINK

ORANGE
& BROWN

NEUTRAL

GREY

Spiced Grey

Add a squirt of spicy orange to an assortment of greys for a pleasing blend of warm and cool colours. A cooler blue-grey provides a contrasting foil to orange, whereas a neutral or warm grey offers a more harmonious vibe.

RED

YELLOW

GREEN

BLUE

VIOLET

PINK

ORANGE
& BROWN

NEUTRAL

GREY

Hot and Cool

Shimmery silver-grey looks hot when paired with deep, lush reds. Play up the drama with generous amounts of black and red. Or, for a palette that has more of a quiet appeal, up the amount of white and grey and limit the darker hues to accents only.

RED

YELLOW

GREEN

BLUE

VIOLET

PINK

ORANGE
& BROWN

NEUTRAL

GREY

Go for Gold

It's common to pair golden yellows with red, orange or brown – fellow warm hues. Break with tradition and use them with grey instead. A yellow and cool grey scheme will have a dynamic quality, whereas a warm grey pairing will feel more relaxed.

RED
YELLOW
GREEN
BLUE
VIOLET
PINK
ORANGE & BROWN
NEUTRAL
GREY

Exquisite Emerald

We tend to associate dark green shades with trees deep in the forest. But instead of pairing these greens with wood-like, bark-brown hues, shake things up and add soft grey instead. It's a surprising combination with a youthful and modern feel.

RED

YELLOW

GREEN

BLUE

VIOLET

PINK

ORANGE
& BROWN

NEUTRAL

GREY

Aqua Accent

Give a grey colour scheme a tropical kick with the addition of aqua. Aqua and turquoise are blue hues that have a touch of yellow in them. This warms them up slightly and prevents the palette from feeling frosty.

RED

YELLOW

GREEN

BLUE

VIOLET

PINK

ORANGE & BROWN

NEUTRAL

GREY

Cool with the Blues

Medium to dark blue-greys are a fantastic alternative to basic black in a colour scheme. Where black can go a bit stern, stuffy or flat, these blue-grey hues offer a softer option. Keep it cool with additions of crisp cobalt and inky indigo.

RED

YELLOW

GREEN

BLUE

VIOLET

PINK

ORANGE & BROWN

NEUTRAL

GREY

Proud as a Peacock

Grey hues are an excellent choice for the base or background layer in a colour scheme. To this neutral foundation you can layer in bright and boisterous colour, such as a bold and beautiful peacock blue.

RED

YELLOW

GREEN

BLUE

VIOLET

PINK

ORANGE & BROWN

NEUTRAL

GREY

Flirting with Grey

For a sophisticated take on sweet pastels, select hues that have a touch of grey in them instead of just white. This gives the colours a muted and neutral quality. The complex character of these tones allows them to be used in a variety of schemes.

RED
YELLOW
GREEN
BLUE
VIOLET
PINK
ORANGE & BROWN
NEUTRAL
GREY

Wink of Pink

This delightful palette of cool blue-greys with a selection of soft pinks is a flirty marriage of colour. It's elegant without being too stuffy or serious. Use it for spaces and occasions when a polished, yet fun vibe is what you're after.

RED

YELLOW

GREEN

BLUE

VIOLET

PINK

ORANGE
& BROWN

NEUTRAL

GREY

Grey Gardens

Many people shy away from grey because they consider it to be a cold, stark and uninviting colour. Here's a grey scheme that is happy, fun and party-ready. Flirty, fruity hues add just enough zest and energy to keep everyone in light spirits.

RED

YELLOW

GREEN

BLUE

VIOLET

PINK

ORANGE & BROWN

NEUTRAL

GREY

Index

Credits

Images for each page are credited clockwise from top left. All images listed in italics have come from **Shutterstock.com**. While every effort has been made to credit contributors, Quarto would like to apologise should there have been any errors or omissions – and would be pleased to make the appropriate correction for future editions of the book.

p. 2 Abode, Living4media.co.uk; *SJ Travel Photo and Video; SvetlanaSF;* The Contemporary Home, Tch.net.; *Sam Aronov;* Henri Del Olmo, Living4media.co.uk; *emin kuliyev; wernerimages; Manamana*
p. 18 *Jalag / Olaf Szczepaniak,* Living4media.co.uk
p. 19 *Alik Mulikov, Maria Sbytova; TatyanaMH; Viktoria Minkova; lemony; lancelot; Sergey Causelove*
p. 20 *photoff*
p. 21 *Ekaterina Pokrovsky; L.F; Elena Elisseeva;* Caroline Guest; *inomasa; Lodimup; Mihail Jershov*
p. 22 *Anatoliy Cherkas*
p. 23 *Xanya69; Sergey Melnikov; Gina Smith;* Steven Morris, Living4media.co.uk; *biggunsband; Joshua Resnick*
p. 24 Lars Ranek, Living4media.co.uk
p. 25 *Jolanta Beinarovica;* Henri Del Olmo, Living4media. co.uk; *claudiodivizia; Kichigin; 3523studio; freya-photographer*
p. 26 *mubus7*
p. 27 *Photographee.eu; tomertu; Ovidiu Hrubaru; sorayafaii; Augustino; Ruth Black*
p. 28 *kqlsm*
p. 29 *MJTH; Joshua Rainey Photography; Tatyana Tomsickova; Catalin Petolea; 1000 Words; VitaliY_Kharin_ and_Maya; filmlandscape*
p. 30 *Ruth Black*
p. 31 *Esat Photography;* Abode, Living4media.co.uk; *Andrey Sarymsakov; prapann; rawmn*
p. 32 *Viktoria Minkova*
p. 33 *sanneberg; FashionStock.com; Douglas Sherman; YSK1;* Great Stock!, Living4media.co.uk; *v.s.anandhakrishna; Evgenialevi*
p. 34 Radoslaw Wojnar, Living4media.co.uk; *daylightistanbul studio*
p. 35 *Miro Vrlik Photography; Jo Green; Nejron Photo; Greg Henry; lightecho; Agnes Kantaruk;* Steven Morris, Living4media.co.uk
p. 36 *Capture Light*
p. 37 *A_Lesik; Ruth Black; blackboard1965; iravgustin; Roman Podvysotskiy; Letterberry*
p. 38 *Ruth Black*
p. 39 *Alex Gukalov; Evgeniya Porechenskaya; webwaffe; Dasha Petrenko; Felix Britanski; Martin Mecnarowski*
p. 40 *lancelot; Roman Sigaev*
p. 41 *Africa Studio; Yassen Hristov,* Living4media.co.uk; *Shana Schnur; Neale Cousland; Daniela Pelazza; Nishihama; Alex Halay*
p. 42 *Irene Barajas; Bronwyn Photo*
p. 43 *Sveta Yaroshuk; Naphat_Jorjee; Vladimir Khirman; Natalia Klenova; Dmitry Abaza; conejota; Volodymyr Leshchenko*
p. 44 *Breadmaker*
p. 45 Frank Sanchez, Living4media.co.uk; *Ruta Production; Bas Meelker; Katsiaryna Yudo; Andre van der Veen; Dmitry Zubarev*
p. 48 *SJ Travel Photo and Video*
p. 49 *Selenit; Dejan Lazarevic; Photographee.eu; Vadim Zholobov;* Caroline Guest; *cdrin; gradi1975; 24Novembers*
p. 50 *FashionStock.com; Africa Studio*
p. 51 *Sophie McAulay; Chris Curtis; aastock; Maria Sbytova; Ruth Black;* Paul Ryan-Goff, Living4media.co.uk
p. 52 *chrishumphreys*
p. 53 *Laitr Keiows; biggunsband; Alexander Image; hofhauser; biggunsband; photo_master2000; Iriana Shiyan*
p. 54 *Dean Pennala*
p. 55 *Dmitry Abaza; Marcel Jancovic; trgowanlock; blackboard1965;* Bratt Décor, brattdecor.com; *zagorodnaya; Joshua Rainey Photography; Africa Studio*
p. 56 *Kamira*
p. 57 *Aleshyn_Andrei; Juli Scalzi; Andrekart Photography; 1000 Words; nioloxs;* Abode, Living4media.co.uk; *IS_ImageSource,* istockphoto.com; *Daniela Pelazza*

p. 58 *Alex Gukalov*
p. 59 *kuzsvetlaya; Alex Gukalov; kregeg; Alex Gukalov; Andrew McDonough; zadirako; milosljubicic; luanateutzi*
p. 60 Steven Morris, Living4media.co.uk
p. 61 *Dmitry_Tsvetkov; Maria Sbytova; Photographee.eu; Ovidiu Hrubaru; daylightistanbul studio; aastock; Maria Sbytova; fabiodevilla*
p. 62 *Stefano Tinti*
p. 63 *ArTono; Photographee.eu; Essential Image Media; ball2be; FashionStock.com;* View Pictures, Living4media.co. uk; *iordani*
p. 64 *FashionStock.com; lancelot*
p. 65 *Karkas; Neirfy; karamysh; WorldWide; Chawalit S; Chris15232*
p. 66 *lancelot*
p. 67 Joshua Rainey Photography; Gianni Sala, Living4media. co.uk; *EpicStockMedia; Gary Yim; Iriana Shiyan; hxdbzxy; Olga Lipatova*
p. 68 *Vincent St. Thomas; Vladimir Melnik*
p. 69 *FashionStock.com;* Caroline Guest; *SunKids; andersphoto; Maxim Kostenko; BRABBU,* brabbu.com
p. 72 *Butterfly Hunter*
p. 73 *Goran Bogicevic; kpatyhka; Nina Struve,* Living4media. co.uk; *c12; Tatyana Borodina; Patryk Kosmider*
p. 74 *TOMO; Tr1sha*
p. 75 *Oleh_Slobodeniuk,* istockphoto.com; Pics On-Line / June Tuesday, Living4media.co.uk; *jesadaphorn; Olga Popkova; Leena Robinson; Anna Ismagilova; Natalia Kirichenko*
p. 76 Abode, Living4media.co.uk
p. 77 *Maria Sbytova; FashionStock.com; hlphoto; PS Prometheus; vitals; Pavel Vakhrushev; liatris; Andrey Sarymsakov*
p. 78 *Viktoriia Chursina*
p. 79 *Jalag / Olaf Szczepaniak,* Living4media.co.uk; *Eco Chic,* ecochic.com.au; *ChameleonsEye; Anna Ismagilova; SvetlanaSF; Artur Synenko; Shana Schnur*
p. 80 *mazur serhiy; Hank Shiffman*
p. 81 *Andreas G. Karelias;* Graham & Brown, Grahambrown. com; *florinstana; Nattle; Chananchida Ch;* Great Stock!, Living4media.co.uk; *Shutterstock.com; Africa Studio*
p. 82 Great Stock!, Living4media.co.uk
p. 83 *Ovidiu Hrubaru; daisydaisy;* Annette & Christian, Living4media.co.uk; *s_karau; sootra; Alina Galieva; Photographee.eu*
p. 84 Graham & Brown, Grahambrown.com; *Maria Sbytova*
p. 85 *Masson;* Brando Cimarosti, Living4media.co.uk; *George Koultouridis; Jacques PALUT; Makela Mona; dfrolovXIII*
p. 86 *MJTH*
p. 87 *Shutterstock.com; Pablo Scapinachis; Iriana Shiyan; Catwalk Photos; Karen Grigoryan; Julia Karo*
p. 88 *pics721*
p. 89 *chrishumphreys; artesiawells; Your Inspiration;* Winfried Heinze, Living4media.co.uk; *Musing Tree Design; Shana Schnur; Kurkul; Rebecca Dickerson*
p. 90 Great Stock!, Living4media.co.uk; *fjphoto*
p. 91 *aastock; Champiofoto; Camille White; Kira Vasilevski; Roman Zhuk; Alex Gukalov*
p. 92 Per Magnus Persson, Living4media.co.uk
p. 93 *Dasha Petrenko; Nata Sha; Halfpoint; ShortPhotos; Dimitrios; Oleksii Nykonchuk;* View Pictures, Living4media. co.uk; *lazyllama*
p. 94 Yassen Hristov, Living4media.co.uk
p. 95 *aastock; adpePhoto; Aleshyn_Andrei; Sam Aronov; eelnosiva; Alex Gukalov; Evgeniya Porechenskaya*
p. 96 *KellyNelson*
p. 97 *Karen Grigoryan; Eva Tigrova; Natalya Osipova;* Paul Ryan-Goff, Living4media.co.uk; *Undivided*
p. 98 Sanderson, Sanderson-uk.com
p. 99 *Jovana Veljkovic; Goran Bogicevic; SJ Allen; Paul Prescott; Difeng Zhu; Evgeny Atamanenko*

p. 100 Mickrick, istockphoto.com
p. 101 *Litvinov; Jacek_Kadaj; MR.LIGHTMAN1975;* Andreas von Einsiedel, Living4media.co.uk; *FashionStock.com; Dash & Albert; Alexander Demyanenko*
p. 102 Great Stock!, Living4media.co.uk; *Dark Moon Pictures*
p. 103 *Sam Aronov; SOMKKU; PAUL ATKINSON; FashionStock.com; Radoslaw Wojnar; 578foot*
p. 104 *Yulia Grigoryeva*
p. 105 *Nata Sha; stockphoto mania; Alla Simacheva; photoagent; lancelot; Milkos*
p. 108 *Evgeniya Porechenskaya*
p. 109 *Andreea Cracium; Evgeniya Porechenskaya; Alex Halay;* Ann Haritonenko; Abode, Living4media.co.uk
p. 110 View Pictures, Living4media.co.uk
p. 111 *Andrey Valerevich Kiselev; Matthew Ennis; Sophie McAulay; Fuyu Liu; Maria Sbytova;* MiaFleur- online homewares, Miafleur.com; *Michael C. Gray;* The Contemporary Home, Tch.net
p. 112 *KUPRYNENKO ANDRII*
p. 113 Ranek, Lars, Living4media.co.uk; *Alexandru Matusciac; PlusONE; MARCHPN; JuliyaNorenko; WorldWide*
p. 114 *flil*
p. 115 *Photographee.eu; Sidhe; Ovidiu Hrubaru; aprilante; imagIN.gr photography; Brum; Chantal de Bruijne*
p. 116 *siculodoc,* iStockphoto.com
p. 117 *Steven Coling; SvetlanaSF; Neale Cousland; StevenRussellSmithPhotos; Evgeniya Porechenskaya;* Jeremy Levine Design, Jeremylevine.com/Flickr The Commons
p. 118 Radoslaw Wojnar, Living4media.co.uk
p. 119 Radoslaw Wojnar; *FashionStock.com; Karniewska; matthewnigel; Stefano Tinti; PlusONE*
p. 120 *Tr1sha*
p. 121 *irbis pictures;* Radoslaw Wojnar, Living4media.co.uk; *leonori; catwalker; Agnes Kantaruk; WorldWide;* Graham & Brown, Grahambrown.com
p. 122 *Stefano Tinti*
p. 123 *Envyligh; Jiri Vaclavek;* Sarah Hogan, Living4media. co.uk; *Maryna Kopylova;* Radoslaw Wojnar, Living4media.co. uk; *infinity21; Jeannette Katzir Photog*
p. 124 *Deborah Kolb*
p. 125 *vinogradnaya; Ovidiu Hrubaru; Prasit Rodphan; Ruth Black; MorganStudio; Prasit Rodphan; MorganStudio*
p. 126 Annette & Christian, Living4media.co.uk; *Christian Bertrand*
p. 127 *Robynrg; Julianna; sirirak kaewgorn; marinomarini; Ruth Black; elitravo*
p. 128 Stuart Cox, Living4media.co.uk; *mates*
p. 129 *InnaFelker; Frolova_Elena; elitravo; Meg Wallace Photography; Ecaterina Petrova; lizabarbiza; Lucy Liu*
p. 130 *Kati Molin*
p. 131 *gephoto; Galina Tcivina; Anna Oleksenko; FashionStock.com; Ecaterina Petrova; Kagual; Elina Leonova*
p. 132 *MillaF*
p. 133 *Jalag / Veronika Stark,* Living4media.co.uk; *HighKey; Pabkov; Victoria Minkova; Ruth Black; arustamova; Anna Antonova; Capture Light*
p. 134 Tara Striano, Living4media.co.uk
p. 135 *sakhorn; Zheng HUANG; Arina P. Habich; Dragon Images; Chris15232; evgeny freeone; AGITA LEIMANE*
p. 136 *WorldWide; Martin Kudrjavcev*
p. 137 Stefan Thurmann, Living4media.co.uk; *conrado;* Idyll Home, Idyllhome.co.uk; *FashionStock.com; B. and E. Dudzinscy; Robert Varga*
p. 138 *Goran Bogicevic*
p. 139 Inge Ofenstein, Living4media.co.uk; *asharkyu; Stefano Tinti; Angela Luchianiuc; Guy Erwood; Dsy;* Winfried Heinze, Living4media.co.uk; *Vikmanis Ints*
p. 140 Mentis Photography, Inc., Living4media.co.uk
p. 141 *BRABBU,* brabbu.com; *Vladzimirska Svyatoslava;* View Pictures, Living4media.co.uk; *Chris15232; Only Fabrizio; blakeley; Percold*
p. 144 *eelnosiva*
p. 145 *wandee007; Anne Kitzman; ariadna de raadt; FashionStock.com; kai keisuke; Yana Godenko; Tom Tom; Igors Rusakovs*
p. 146 *Alex Gukalov*

p. 147 *Elena Rostunova; Abode, Living4media.co.uk; Ruslan Iefremov; Tom Lester; crystalfoto; Discovod; Miro Vrlik Photography; Castka; KOBRIN PHOTO*
p. 148 *KPG_Payless; totojang1977*
p. 149 *Belovodchenko Anton; piccaya; Joshua Rainey Photography; Andrea Haase; Henri Del Olmo, Living4media. co.uk; Africa Studio; Maria Sbytova; Eve81*
p. 150 *lancelot*
p. 151 *FashionStock.com; Magdanatka; wernerimages; FashionStock.com; Illya Vinogradov; irbis pictures; ChameleonsEye*
p. 152 Simon Maxwell Photography, Living4media.co.uk; *Petar Djordjevic*
p. 153 Tapetenfabrik Gebr. Rasch GmbH & Co. KG, rasch-tapete.de; *Ausf; Deatonphotos; Africa Studio; Sam Aronov; tymonko; Tom Lester*
p. 154 *AdrianC*
p. 155 *Phatthanit; Dmitry Abaza; Elena Rostunova; melis; Jayne Chapman; Annette & Christian, Living4media.co.uk; marylooo; PonomarenkoNataly*
p. 156 Bärbel Miebach, Living4media.co.uk
p. 157 *IVASHstudio; TorriPhoto; Ovidiu Hrubaru; Tr1sha; Wichudapa; Champiofoto; Juta*
p. 158 *Alla Simacheva; Massel_Marina*
p. 159 *FashionStock.com; locrifa; StacieStaufffSmith Photos; JMS Splash Photography; Oksana Shufrych; smartape; Evgheni Lachi; WorldWide*
p. 160 *Shebeko*
p. 161 *dragi52; Shebeko; Shebeko; A_Lesik; Seqoya; Dobermaraner; Oleksandr Lipko*
p. 162 *Michael Warwick*
p. 163 *Jakkrit Orrasri; Kachergina; Karin Jaehne; matthewnigel; TorriPhoto; Still AB*
p. 164 Evangelos Paterakis, Living4media.co.uk; *maoyunping*
p. 165 *Yana Godenko; Mariya Volik; Ovidiu Hrubaru; Melica; Sergio Stakhnyk; Carpet Vista, Coloured Vintage and Nepal Original, CarpetVista.com; rehanq*
p. 168 *Natalia Van Doninck*
p. 169 *Paul Matthew Photography; Lucy Liu; Joshua Rainey Photography; IBL Bildbyra AB / Angelica, Söderberg, Living4media.co.uk; Asaf Eliason; AppStock; tanger*
p. 170 *Neale Cousland*
p. 171 *Evgeniy Porechenskaya; Everything; NinaMalyna; Cecilia Möller, Living4media.co.uk; Ecaterina Petrova; WeStudio*
p. 172 Cecilia Möller, Living4media.co.uk
p. 173 *locrifa; Evgeniya Porechenskaya; Gina Smith; elitravo; popovartem.com; Lim Yong Hian; Tarzhanova; emin kuliyev*
p. 174 *Yassen Hristov, Living4media.co.uk*
p. 175 *Ovidiu Hrubaru; Ruth Black; Forewer; wandee007; D_D; Victoria Minkova; aastock*
p. 176 *Ruth Black; Marilyn Barbone*
p. 177 Syl Loves, Living4media.co.uk; *akayuki; Alena Ozerova; All About Space; Ruth Black;* Tom Meadow, Living4media.co.uk; *Kaspars Grinvalds*
p. 178 *Odrida*
p. 179 *Anna-Mari West; FXQuadro; CLS Design; Det-anan; Andrekart Photography; Syl Loves, Living4media.co.uk*
p. 180 *Ruth Black;* Paul Rich Studio
p. 181 *danielo; Agnes Kantaruk; AS Inc; IBL Bildbyra AB / Peter Ericsson, Living4media.co.uk; Andrii Kobryn; Ruth Black*
p. 182 Annette & Christian, Living4media.co.uk; *Shell114*
p. 183 Art Hide - Stylist Tess Beagley and Photographer Carrie Young, Arthide.com; *Fotokon; Maria lial; cameilia; iDecorate; idecorateshop; carlo dapino; Beto Chagas*
p. 184 *kazoka*
p. 185 *Ovidiu Hrubaru; Photographee.eu;* MiaFleur- online homewares. Styling and photography: Amelia and Jacqui Brooks, Miafleur.com; *Magdanatka; Vladislav Plotnikov; Oleg Elena Tovkach; vinogradnaya*
p. 186 *Yana Godenko; Wig*
p. 187 *Miro Vrlik Photography; Robert Fesus; Vitalii Tiagunov; Evgeniya Porechenskaya; elitravo; kostrez; Sergey Chirkov*
p. 188 *Robert Varga*
p. 189 *FashionStock.com; SATHIANPONG PHOOKIT; John Copland; Dmitry Abaza; OmiStudio; Hteam; vinogradnaya*
p. 192 *Chris15232*
p. 193 *FashionStock.com; Andrey Kucheruk; Karen Grigoryan;* Bärbel Miebach, Living4media.co.uk; *Niradj; TOMO*
p. 194 *anat chant*
p. 195 *bostonphotographer; David Tadevosian; Patrick Foto; Manamana; Masson; Nata Sha; Debbi Gerdt; photobyjoy*

p. 196 Annette & Christian, Living4media.co.uk
p. 197 *Lifebrary; Goran Bogicevic; FashionStock.com; c12; Alex Andrei; aastock*
p. 198 Bratt Décor, brattdecor.com
p. 199 *Jodie Johnson; goldenjack; Yuriy Kuzakov; Henrique Daniel Araujo; aastock; Ovidiu Hrubaru*
p. 200 *catwalker*
p. 201 *Rade Kovac; Gianni Sala; FashionStock.com; Anastasiia Kryvenok; Nadya Korobkova; Alexander Tihonov; Alinute Silzeviciute*
p. 202 Annette & Christian, Living4media.co.uk
p. 203 *Breadmaker; Alexandru Matusciac; 3523studio; Chris15232; Ruth Black; Oleksandr Rostov*
p. 204 Tapetenfabrik Gebr. Rasch GmbH & Co. KG, rasch-tapete.de
p. 205 *aastock;* Wayne Vincent, Living4media.co.uk; *Robsonphoto; taniavolobueva; Dmitry Abaza; Neale Cousland; kees luiten*
p. 206 *Maleo*
p. 207 *Eric Limon; Shana Schnur; Ashwin; Andrey Armyagov; Winfried Heinze, Living4media.co.uk; Alexandre Zveiger*
p. 208 Rene van der Hulst, Living4media.co.uk
p. 209 *aastock; Radonja Srdanovic; Anastasiia Kryvenok; FashionStock.com; KULISH VIKTORIIA; Ann Haritonenko; Everything*
p. 210 *polusvet; IVASHstudio*
p. 211 *Max Smolyar; Lukasz Zandecki, Living4media.co.uk; MIKHAIL MAKOVKIN; Ulrika Ekblom, Living4media.co.uk; VOJTa Herout; c12*
p. 212 Simon Scarboro, Living4media.co.uk
p. 213 *Arina P. Habich; Photographee.eu; Karen Grigoryan; Guas; Marion Abada; nico99*
p. 214 *aprilante*
p. 215 Wayne Vincent, Living4media.co.uk; *Superlime; Natalia Priadilshchikova; bezikus; kregeg; L.F*
p. 216 Radoslaw Wojnar, Living4media.co.uk
p. 217 *Sufi; Volodymyr Shulevskyy; Alexandre Zveiger; Photographee.eu; Aleshyn_Andrei; Shutterstock.com*
p. 218 *Alexandre Zveiger*
p. 219 *Miro Vrlik Photography; Alexandre Zveiger; IVASHstudio; Ruth Black; Victoria_Fox;* View Pictures, Living4media.co.uk
p. 220 Great Stock!, Living4media.co.uk
p. 221 *Kaspars Grinvalds; Kateryna Mostova; Syda Productions; arustamova; Tr1sha; Gordana Sermek; StrelaStudio*
p. 222 *Branko Jovanovic*
p. 223 Jalag / Angelika Lorenzen, Living4media.co.uk; *Ovidiu Hrubaru; paultarasenko; Tata Mamai; WorldWide; 5 second Studio*
p. 224 Luci italiane. Evi Style by Stefano Mandruzzato, Luciitaliane.com; *Irina Tischenko*
p. 225 *indira's work; Alexandre Zveiger; Diego Schtutman; ThitareeS; Svetlana Lukienko; Wiratchai wansamngam*
p. 228 Annette & Christian, Living4media.co.uk
p. 229 *bikeriderlondon; aprilante; Ovidiu Hrubaru; Maglara; Eric Limon; Chantal de Bruijne*
p. 230 *LarisaS*
p. 231 *Miro Vrlik Photography; sl_photo; Maria Sbytova; Sisacorn; lkpro; Anna Subbotina; plepraisaeng; Melanie Hobson*
p. 232 *Santiago Cornejo*
p. 233 *KUPRYNENKO ANDRII; michaeljung; eelnosiva; Alex Gukalov; Ulyana Khorunzha; lev radin; Faiz Zaki*
p. 234 View Pictures, Living4media.co.uk
p. 235 *blueeyes; Ann Haritonenko; MNStudio; Ana Photo; attila; eelnosiva*
p. 236 Lukasz Zandecki, Living4media.co.uk
p. 237 *Caroline Guest; triocean; Agnes Kantaruk; USAart studio; Dmitry Abaza; Joshua Rainey Photography; Anastasiia Kryvenok*
p. 238 *Ingrid Maasik*
p. 239 *Alexandre Zveiger; Gerasia; Yuliya Yafimik; Sussie Bell, Living4media.co.uk; Iriana Shiyan; Lucy Baldwin*
p. 240 *piccaya; avers*
p. 241 Sanderson, Sanderson-uk.com; *FashionStock.com; Alberto P; Photo Africa; Tr1sha;* Graham & Brown, Grahambrown.com
p. 242 Bernard Touillon, Living4media.co.uk
p. 243 *Kartinkin77; Olga Lipatova; Vladzimirska Svyatoslava; Jay Petersen; ShortPhotos; bikeriderlondon*
p. 244 *All About Space; Alex Gukalov*
p. 245 *Kagual;* Brando Cimarosti, Living4media.co.uk; *Stefano Tronci; Aleksie; Kenneth Keifer; Mathe, Dorottya; JuliyaNorenko*

p. 246 Rachael Smith, Living4media.co.uk
p. 247 *design.at.krooogle; FashionStock.com; WorldWide; Karen Grigoryan; WorldWide;* BRABBU, brabbu.com
p. 248 *Alex Gukalov*
p. 249 *kuvona; Anatoliy Cherkas;* Great Stock!, Living4media. co.uk; *Alex Gukalov; Sophie McAulay; Ovidiu Hrubaru; syrotkin; Marilyn Barbone*
p. 250 Guy Bouchet, Living4media.co.uk
p. 251 *IVASHstudio; Nikolas_jkd; Santiago Cornejo; Viktoriia Chursina; zhekoss; Owl_photographer; Studio ART; Bogdan Sonjachnyj*
p. 252 Rachael Smith, Living4media.co.uk
p. 253 IN-SPACES, In-spaces.com; *Radoslaw Lecyk; pongnathee kluaythong; Andrekart Photography; Photographee.eu; brodtcast; Sam Aronov*
p. 254 Great Stock!, Living4media.co.uk
p. 255 *KUPRYNENKO ANDRII; Your Inspiration; Dragon Images; All About Space; FashionStock.com*
p. 256 Annette & Christian, Living4media.co.uk; *traumschoen*
p. 257 *Pavel Sytsko; Iriana Shiyan; Alexandre Zveiger; Ovidiu Hrubaru; rehanq; Ozgur Coskun*
p. 260 *José-Luis Hausmann,* Living4media.co.uk
p. 261 *hifashion; PlusONE; Odrida; Jaros;* Idyll Home, idyllhome.co.uk
p. 262 *gifted*
p. 263 Boca do Lobo, Bocadolobo.com; *Algirdas Gelazius; Alexandre Zveiger; pbombaert; LIU ANLIN; Henri Del Olmo, Living4media.co.uk*
p. 264 Annette & Christian, Living4media.co.uk
p. 265 *GoodMood Photo; Sam Aronov; 2M media; Africa Studio; jan1982*
p. 266 *Marko Poplasen*
p. 267 Tulikivi Kide 2 Fireplace White by Tulikivi2012 - Own work. Licensed under CC BY-SA 3.0 via Wikimedia Commons, Commons.wikimedia.org/wiki/File:Tulikivi_Kide_2_Fireplace_ White.jpg#/media/File:Tulikivi_Kide_2_Fireplace_White.jpg; *paultarasenko; saschanti17; Jodie Johnson; WorldWide; Vladzimirska Svyatoslava*
p. 268 *stockernumber2,*
p. 269 *lev radin;* Peter Kooijman, Living4media.co.uk; *Anna Hoychuk; melis; T30 Gallery; pics721; ladie_c*
p. 270 *Alexandre Zveiger*
p. 271 *chrishumphreys; Ben Bryant; Tinxi; Oleg Malyshev; FreeBirdPhotos; Chris15232; Lorna Roberts; NinaMalyna*
p. 272 View Pictures, Living4media.co.uk; *Tinxi*
p. 273 *happydancing;* Yvonne von Oswald, Living4media.co. uk; *Antonius Egurnov; WorldWide;* BRABBU, brabbu.com; *TaraPatta; hifashion*
p. 274 Peter Kooijman, Living4media.co.uk
p. 275 *Andrey Bayda; Maria Sbytova; FashionStock.com; All About Space; iOso; IVASHstudio*
p. 276 Great Stock!, Living4media.co.uk
p. 277 Annette & Christian, Living4media.co.uk; *FashionStock.com; Maria Sbytova; SvetlanaSF; All About Space; indira's work; PlusONE*
p. 278 Radoslaw Wojnar, Living4media.co.uk; *Neangell*
p. 279 *FashionStock.com;* Radoslaw Wojnar, Living4media. co.uk; Simone Becchetti, Stocksy; *fiphoto;* Interior Design: Builders Design, Builder: KB Home, Buildersdesign.com; *Andrei Zveaghintev*
p. 280 Tom Meadow, Living4media.co.uk
p. 281 *Mikhail_Kayl; karamysh; WorldWide; Elena Schweitzer; Yulia Grigoryeva; FashionStock.com; David Papazian*
p. 282 Great Stock!, Living4media.co.uk
p. 283 *PlusONE; Chris15232; Andreja Donko; Agnes Kantaruk; mythja; Nata Sha*
p. 284 Emily May, Gohausgo.com
p. 285 *Photographee.eu;* Emily May, Gohausgo.com; *SARYMSAKOV ANDREY; patsy&ulla,* Living4media.co.uk; *Photographee.eu; Nattle; AC Manley*